On Productivity

The Collective Wisdom of the

Most Efficient Man Alive

by Ari Meisel

Printed in the United States of America

First Edition

Copyright © 2021 Ari Meisel

ISBN: 9798731416870

Table of Contents

Foreword

I am a cynic.

Ante contemptus est inquisitio or "Contempt prior to investigation" was pretty much going to be my next tattoo. And so it was, with this remarkably closed mind, that I began my professional relationship with Ari Meisel and Productivity.

I needed work. He was an old friend who had a virtual assistant company. He said I had to go through the hiring process anyway even though I reminded him that... um, we were old friends. But I was not to worry, according to Ari. Things were going to be pretty straightforward.

Not.

As I said, I needed the work. So I found a flattering (read: wrinkle-diminishing) spot at my kitchen window. Put my hair in a messy bun the way the kids were doing it then. Did all the fake exercises to see if I could solve problems on the fly. Then proceeded to say terrible words in rapid succession, to get a damn video to upload to YouTube, which I'd never done. I got the job.

Everyone was a whole lot younger than me and had next-level productivity vocabularies. I understood very little about how things worked, and it didn't matter. The Buddhist monk Pema Chodron tells us to find in this kind of situation "the wisdom of no escape." When you have no choice, you figure it out. Productivity Win #1. Constraints are beneficial.

But with each win came the requisite mistakes.

Mistake #1: Nodding knowingly on team huddles over Zoom (we used Zoom way before it was cool, btw). I wish I had just asked the question and copped to my ignorance. I would have gotten an instructive answer and probably would have helped someone else who didn't know what the hell was going on either but didn't have the courage to ask.

Still, I built up my remote-gig-hustle sea legs. Despite my overly judgmental attitude, I was able to chalk up Productivity Win #2 when I figured out my Peak Time (6–9 A.M.). Yes, there's an app for it. Ari made one. Because, of course, he did.

I knew I was making solid progress when one morning I looked at my laptop. I had fifteen open tabs, and I didn't feel nauseous. I flew around Slack, spitballing ideas, attaching files, dropping lit AF gifs for any occasion. It felt good.

Client passwords were safe in Dashlane. My Trello boards were a Kanban thing of beauty, showcasing both velocity and a chill graphic vibe. I could feel myself falling in love with Canva, even though I wasn't ready for the paid membership. Take it slow, Amy. Take it slow. Wait until it drops an Instagram integration.

Then Ari decided to go out on his own.

I was giddy when he asked me to sit at the cool kids' table and be part of the nascent team he was putting together for Less Doing. But now, there was nowhere to hide. I couldn't play the helpless old lady card anymore and get someone else to do the hard parts of content work. You know, like trending hashtags (like why is that even important?) and speaking truth to power about pervasive toxic masculinity in LinkedIn videos. So I bought blue-blocking Warby Parkers and subscribed to the HubSpot newsletter.

It seemed like every other day Ari sent a shiny new platform for me to use in my pursuit of streamlined, on-brand messaging. And he did it with a caveat to the rest of the team.

"No one is allowed to help Amy. No one."

Now your first reaction is probably quite similar to my initial reaction.

"What a d*&K."

But that is where you are wrong.

Mr. Miyagi was teaching me the most valuable productivity lesson.

I bashed around my keyboard. Squinted at error messages. Bristled at the failure sound that a Mac makes when it knows you're trying to go someplace you'll regret, like Vegas in August.

"I'll show him," I mumbled. I can shorten backlinks. Stock photo choices are not going to be the end of me.

I sent the work back to Ari for approval or just pulled the Level 6 trigger (see page 65) and didn't even ask. "I did it," I'd say, hitting return with equal parts spite and pride.

Ari said to me soon thereafter. "You know why I told everyone not to help you with this stuff, right?"

"Because you're a d*&k?"

"No, a-hole. Smarter people than you and me built these platforms," he said smiling. "You couldn't possibly break anything. I wanted you to get in there, make mistakes, mess around, and build up your confidence. Because that muscle memory never disappears."

Productivity Win #3: You can't break it. Just do it.

It's getting harder to remember that woman who was so afraid of change and innovation, that wildly unproductive human who wasted so much time. I don't miss her very much, and we only really get reacquainted when a new season of *The Crown* drops.

My success with a productive life is not measured by the sheer volume of work I produced for Ari or its quality. That's kind of a

BS metric. It's that he taught me how to use time efficiently enough to have time. Time to take care of my children, my health, my home, and my burgeoning political and literary pursuits.

He showed me how to build a life to be proud of—and I am.

If I can do it, anyone can.

--Amy Randall

An Introduction

The chase to lead a productive life is extraordinarily misguided and, for many people, downright disheartening.

It might be because the way we define productivity today is a holdover from a time when Japanese management terms like Kaizen, Kanban, and the Five Whys, were all the rage.

Back then, when shoulder pads and Brioni suits roamed the earth, productivity meant producing more. How productive you were was about how much you made, a quantifiable number of goods, services, or profits.

Efficiency, or jidoka, was defined as producing the most with the least. The most efficient person (or process) was the one who did the most, got the most done, and created the most while using the least amount of resources.

These constructs are totally applicable if you're talking about Toyota production, but not so much if you're talking about entrepreneurs. So, I'd say it's way past time to update the notion of productivity: its meaning, intent, and goals.

We've got a lot to cover. Stay hydrated.

First, productivity is the wrong thing to pursue. Productivity, efficiency, and effectiveness are all byproducts of a change that takes place internally. They are not an end result. But "mindset" is not a static or absolute concept either. It's not a lockstep prescription for success. "Getting in the right mindset" seems to mean we all have to think a certain way. That's nonsense. It's personal.

For example, you could have all the tech in the world, all the tools that I recommend, like Trello, Voxer, Slack, Intercom, and Zapier. But if the tool is not in sync with the way your mind works, you will not become more productive, efficient, or effective. You'll get frustrated.

Technology only amplifies habits. If you have good habits, technology helps you make them better. If you have bad habits, the tech will make them worse. I have seen some Trello boards that are straight-up masterpieces, and I've seen Trello boards that are the technological equivalent of my mother's kitchen junk drawer.

Technology does not have the power to make you productive. Only you do.

I think the goal, the shift, the mindset, and needs come from a greater appreciation of effectiveness. By definition, this means you're successful in producing the desired outcome.

If it works for you, you're being effective.

Look, there are very well established productivity systems out there, like *The Eisenhower Matrix* and *Getting Things Done* and *Less Doing*. Just because they don't work for you, it doesn't mean you have a productivity problem.

Conversely, if you have something that's working well for you, it doesn't mean you can't improve it. But getting off the winning horse because there's another horse that has more followers on Instagram is definitely not a good plan.

So why do we have this thing about being more productive? It's pure ego.

I did more.

I work less.

I made more.

I sleep better.

I am more right.

Did you know James Patterson has written, at last count, 147 books in his career? Obviously, he's extremely productive. Are they all works of art? No way. But it's still pretty impressive. However, this measurement of success by volume, whether it's books or brainstorms, comes at a cost.

Producing more costs something, and I'm not just talking about money. I can't think of any situation where producing more costs less. Now the ratio may change, obviously, but for each incremental unit of productivity, you may have a smaller, incremental unit of cost, and as productivity increases, costs do too.

Those costs are most damaging between our ears, where stress and a feeling of being overwhelmed can breed so easily. Too many entrepreneurs I've met freak the f*ck out because they're not productive enough. Most of the time, they compare themselves against a yardstick that doesn't exist or have any relevance in the real world.

So if you're doing that, stop.

Also, no matter who you are and what position you're in, feeling overwhelmed can undoubtedly come from things over which we have no control. An illness in the family or a child with learning disabilities or the death of a loved one causes such feelings and should never be discounted, ignored, or glossed over.

But when somebody says they are overwhelmed because they have too many emails in their inbox; they have too many research articles to read; they have too many reports to write; well, that is a hundred percent about mindset.

You don't need a single tool or a single piece of technology. You might not even need electricity to eradicate the feeling of being overwhelmed. All you need to do is change your relationship with your expectations. When it comes to the actual pursuit, ask yourself, Are you successful in producing the desired result?

Now, of course, to have the answer requires that you know the desired results. Many people don't. They bury themselves in a never-ending state of busyness to create a sense of urgency—and become overwhelmed as a result. They wear it as a badge of honor all the while wasting time, resources, and energy on themselves and others.

Here's a choice worth pondering. Imagine that I gave you $10 and told you that you can invest in this thing, which will provide you with a $20 return in one month's time, or you can invest in this other thing, which will give you a thousand dollars return after 10 years. The one you'd pick is a no-brainer, right? If the desired outcome is to make as much money as possible with your $10, you'd choose number two.

Then why do so many people take a dollar and say, "I'm going to find something that's going to make me $1.15? Then I'm going to take another dollar and find another thing that makes me $1.15. I will invest in things all day long, and at the end of the day, I'll probably make $1.15." It may seem hyperbolic, but I think that reasoning is pretty widespread. It's no one's fault. We have a culture that has created this relentless pursuit or more, even if the end result is less.

Big law firms are a great example. New lawyers are supposed to bill as many hours as humanly possible, with the goal being the more, the better. But that's not about being effective.

Here's one more example.

Let's say the world is working on a vaccine. Would you rather one group of scientists spend years and years and years trying thousands of different combinations to hopefully one day five, six, seven years in the future, get a vaccine that is 80% effective? Or would it be better to slow down, divide up the work, and have each research group identify 20 possible combinations, and then spend six months testing those to get a solution that's 98% effective?

We can do that in everyday life.

It comes down to doing the right thing at the right time for the right reason—and nothing else.

The Landmines of an Unproductive Life

I'm going to start with the bad stuff, the stuff we don't want to talk about, the secrets and lies we tell ourselves about why things aren't going more smoothly.

The four horsemen of an unproductive life, in no particular order, are:

Procrastination

Disorganization

Decision Paralysis

Rudderless Teams

So gird your loins and look at the next few pages as a vigorous exfoliation or a seasonal cleanse but with results that go deeper and last way longer.

Procrastination sucks. Akrasia is worse.

Relax.

Everybody deals with procrastination at some point, some more than others.

The most beleaguered among us go so far as to identify themselves as "Procrastinators" with a capital P. It's a slippery slope. This negative self-identification gives Procrastinators permission to bail on almost everything and their excuses only exacerbate the distress and stress, contributing to further procrastination.

Research has shown that there are four cognitive distortions (irrational thoughts) that are symptomatic of procrastination.

Overestimating the time left to perform a task.

"I've got days to get it done."

Underestimating the time required to complete it.

"It will take me ten minutes."

Associating motivation with success.

"If I liked doing spreadsheets, I'd be so much better at them."

Believing it's necessary to be in the right mood.

"I just need to get in the zone first."

Sound familiar?

Ultimately, procrastination is rooted in psychology. So it's not going to be solved by installing the latest app. It's not going to be solved by hiring a great assistant. If you genuinely want to solve procrastination, you need to address and identify why you procrastinate in the first place.

Fear tops the list.

But what exactly are we afraid of? Some people are fearful of getting it wrong. People aren't going to like it. We're going to look foolish.

Some people have a fear of getting it right, a fear of success. If they get it right and get accolades, they get elevated. Now all of a sudden, they have more responsibility. They've raised the bar. There's more pressure. And so they avoid it.

Whatever the reason, you need to be aware of something way more insidious than procrastination, and more likely, the thing from which you are suffering.

It's called akrasia.

It's been a preoccupation of big brain thinkers since the Peloponnesian War when Plato, Socrates, and Aristotle all weighed in on this pillar of moral philosophy. The ancient Greek translation is "lack of self-control," but it is now used as a general term for the phenomenon known as weakness of will, or why we act contrary to our judgment about the best course of action.

The critical difference between akrasia and procrastination is that with procrastination you've decided to do something. You're going to do that report that you have to write up. You're going to put out a blog post. You're going to your in-laws for three weeks. You've identified what you're going to do, and you've made a plan to do it.

But now, you are putting active roadblocks in your way, those roadblocks being fear or perfectionism, which is just procrastination in a different suit. Still, you've made a decision, and now you're simply and actively stopping yourself from doing it.

So with procrastination, you need to get out of your own way.

On the other hand, akrasia is where you know you should do something, but you don't have the will or the fortitude to put a plan in place to make it happen.

Aristotle (the winner of the big brain argument) said that it is natural for humans to have akrasia. We often find ourselves motivated by impetuosity or passion, which can cause a lapse in reason. It diverts a person from what they believe to be the right actions. Damaging? Sure. Natural? Absolutely.

So I'll give you a concrete example: dieting and losing weight.

Over the last month or so, I have been eating pretty poorly. I haven't been eating the best stuff. I've been snacking a lot, even having bowls of cereal at 11 P.M. Uncharacteristic for me, but it happens.

I haven't seen many shifts in my body, but there have been shifts in my mood and ability to be effective. There's no question I'm not operating optimally. So for the last two weeks, I've been telling myself, stop snacking, stop eating like that. Stop snacking, stop, stop, stop.

And sure enough, the more I tell myself to stop, the more likely I am to do it. Until four days ago, when I realized that I was suffering from akrasia, I wasn't procrastinating about making a change. I was suffering because I had no plan.

And I had to remind myself, "What works for you, Ari? Oh right, intermittent fasting." Now, we don't have to get into the science of intermittent fasting. My point here is that it's a structure that works for me.

So I went back to intermittent fasting. It was 6:30 at night. I had just finished dinner with my family. And I said, okay, I'm going to start right now. I'm going to follow the 6/18 plan—6 hours of eating; 18 hours of not eating—which is what I've done before. I've stuck to it for several days now.

Now, if I had made that plan and I was still saying, "Oh, I'll start tomorrow. I'll start next week. I know we've got the birthday party coming up, so I'll do it after that," that would be procrastination. So don't make the confusing mistake of thinking that you're suffering from procrastination when it's akrasia. Look at the things you're doing, the stuff you feel are scenarios of procrastination, and ask yourself, Do you have a plan? Because if there is no plan, then you are suffering from akrasia.

Ultimately the character trait that makes somebody procrastination-proof is doing what you say you're going to do, which of course requires that you identify with a goal and then follow through on it. Even if you say it out loud to yourself, in the car, in the kitchen, walking the dog, say what you're going to do. Then do what you said you would do.

Now there's one caveat to procrastination.

It can be an essential tool because when you get to the point where you're no longer a procrastinator, as I can confidently say, I am. It doesn't happen to me except when it does. And when it does, I look at it and remind myself that when I do procrastinate, it's my body and my mind telling me that this is something that I really should not be doing, which is a whole lot better than me telling myself I should do it but just don't want to. Feel me?

17

Once you begin this process, you have a hope of unraveling the reasons that make you into somebody who procrastinates, and then you can start to unpack those.

And you could totally start doing this today. Like, right now is good.

Disorganization is an Inside Job

Albert Einstein famously pointed out that "if a cluttered desk is a sign of a cluttered mind, of what, then, is an empty desk a sign?"

Now I'm not here to Marie Kondo your work environment. I want to talk about the disorganization inside your head that may be keeping you from becoming a more effective person, no matter what the hell your desk looks like.

And it all starts with focus—or lack thereof.

So, what do you imagine optimal focus looks like?

Is focus sitting at an empty desk with headphones on listening to binaural beats after taking a nootropic to get your brain functioning the way you want?

Is it drinking yerba mate tea while standing at a standing desk writing the most epic blog posts you've ever written without stopping for two hours?

Is it wandering through a snowy glade, immersed in a whole sense experience of oneness with all, grateful you're wearing a merino wool base layer?

Conjured images are a strong flex for bio-wellness influencers who live off-grid with their rescue dogs, and geo-thermal Wi-Fi, but good luck achieving that in the real world. If you have a family or responsibilities that require you to be present for others, this made-for-Instagram construct isn't going to work.

It sounds a little bit judgmental. It's not intentional. But focus techniques that work for a specific subset of people will never work for a larger percentage of the population. And if they don't work for the larger populus, then people end up feeling like they are doing something wrong.

I call it #focusshaming. Would love to get that trending.

Think about it. Consider the following three items:

"Oh, I tried the *Getting Things Done* method. It didn't work for me. I'm just such a lost cause."

"I bought *The Full Focus Planner* But I'm such a mess. I don't even know where it is."

"I'm too overwhelmed and distracted most days to even think about listening to a Tim Ferriss podcast.

Do any of these ring a bell with you? If so, let it go.

There is nothing fundamentally wrong with you. It's not a character flaw you haven't figured out yet. It's just another example of throwing enormous amounts of money and effort into solving a problem before you know what the actual problem is.

Here's how I see it.

We have a minimal window within which to focus because the brain works best in sprints. It doesn't work so well in marathon sessions. I imagine it's a vestige of our hunting-gathering beginnings, where bursts of activity, like fleeing, kept us alive one more day.

This sprinting notion is an integral part of the Pomodoro Technique™ where you're working in 25-minute sprints. The method has unimpeachable validity, but even 25 minutes might be pushing it for some people.

Finding our lost or underdeveloped focus requires flexibility. It's not easy to do.

We have to train for and practice with it because the problem we face is the inability to execute a routine, even if we want to. So the best-laid plans get thrown out, and all we're left with is resentment and regret. And that sucks.

Some people have massively complex two-hour morning routines. But if they wake up and their spouse is sick, and the kids are learning virtually, and someone forgot to put almond milk in the Instacart, well, you see what I mean.

Or maybe somebody sits down to write a blog post. They're planning on devoting 25 minutes to it. Then, seven minutes into it, they get interrupted by a disgruntled client call. Oh well, it's just shot.

We need to get things done in the time we have to do it. Again, I'm not trying to oversimplify things, but there is no benefit to us fighting against the inevitable and the unchangeable. Work within the constraints we have, the constraints we are given, or the constraints we self-impose.

Acceptance is the key to flexibility.

And speaking of flexibility, can we discuss multitasking for a minute?

It's technically known as context switching, but many of us understand it as multitasking, which no one does well. I'm totally prepared to fight you on this, btw.

Multitasking damages our ability to get things done, saps our energy levels, and wrecks our willpower. But again, it's completely unavoidable. You're going to be in a situation where you're working on something, and you have to jump over and answer an email or field a question.

So flexibility is being agile, being able to roll with the punches.

Mike Tyson loved to say, "Everybody has a plan until they get punched in the mouth."

Every one of us gets proverbially punched in the mouth multiple times a day. You have a choice. You can lie down, or you can get back up and do something about it.

Communication Breakdown

So the number one culprit, the true enemy to focus is communication.

Communication often happens at the wrong time, in the wrong place, for the wrong reason. One of the main things I teach in The Replaceable Founder™ methodology is something we call a "Communication SOP," where you're intentional about the types of tools you use and for which types of communication.

You have one tool for internal communication and a different tool for external communication. You have a separate tool that bridges the gap between the two, and you have an additional tool for things that need to get done. You don't discuss things that need to get done in a communication tool. They belong in a project management setting. You don't use an internal tool for client work.

Next, it would help if you decided what is urgent and what is not.

For me, the definition of urgent communication is something that necessitates an interruption. I will do absolutely anything I can to avoid disruption because interruptions have a lasting effect. You get knocked out of your focus, and it takes you a while to get back into it. Think about how long the traffic on the Long Island Expressway takes to get back up to speed after a car accident.

So if urgent things are the things you want to be interrupted for, how do you control urgencies? You have to be intentional. You have to communicate to those around you precisely and specifically what urgent looks like. Because trust me, urgent is in the eye of the beholder.

The thing that is urgent to one person is rarely urgent to somebody else.

It's a scenario you typically see in an office setting with new people. Say something happened with a client that seems like a big deal. They freak out. They email you, and you don't respond to their email immediately. So then they text you, and you don't respond to a text message. So then they call you. And then, if we were in an office setting, they come down the hall and knock on your door.

You let out an audible sigh and answer the question—you firefight instead of fireproof.

Now I completely understand that firefighting is a whole lot sexier than fireproofing. Firefighting is heroic, immediate and adrenal producing. Fireproofing is more Dad Bod work. It's necessary, and will probably save more lives, but no one ever got a rush from switching out the smoke detector batteries.

24

You and your company need fireproof systems and processes, so firefighting doesn't have to be a daily part of your culture.

Focus is about avoiding interruptions, and avoiding interruptions is about proactively designing a communication protocol around you to support both big and small amounts of "you time."

Hacking your calendar

I have a full calendar, and maybe that's surprising for people who know me and know what I do. The cool part is I don't have a single call scheduled on my calendar.

In fact, I have 16 different calendars on my Google account. There's my wife's calendar, my four kids' calendars—various holidays and events. The sales and marketing calendar for my business and the calendar feed from a service that provides continuing education classes for my EMT work.

You might think that this sounds busy and overwhelming. Nope. The critical element here is that I'm the one filling it. I'm the one controlling my time, what I do, where I do it, and how I do it. So if it's not on my calendar, it's not happening.

Say somebody wants to meet with me synchronously or have a call. Now, whether I say it out loud or not, my mindset is "Let me see if I can free up a slot for that" rather than "I'm not sure. Pick any time you want, and we'll send fifteen emails back and forth to nail down a time."

While I'm a big fan of scheduling apps, because you can still control those time slots, this particular mindset is different. It's about being *intentional*. When it comes to being more effective, intention is the operative word. The way we communicate. The way we manage projects. The way we run processes and optimize them. You have to be intentional.

Unfortunately, too many people are passengers in their own lives.

How you manage your time, your energy, and your resources determines whether you'll be a passenger or driver in your own life.

Many people use their calendars as an agenda that other people fill for them. Nobody should be starting the week with an empty calendar because come Monday morning there will be 15 requests for sales calls, and pitch meetings, and team huddles. Suddenly, the calendar fills up, and by Friday, sure, stuff got done, but was it effective stuff? Were you in charge of any of it? Or did it just happen, like it always does?

Now I've seen people go so far as to put in a block from 11:00 P.M. to 7:00 A.M., marked "sleep." I don't do that personally, but you can certainly do that. It's a good practice.

There is an interesting argument for scheduling sex with your spouse. And as unromantic as that might sound, research has found that to some people, it's simply a promise to make time for one another.

It doesn't mean that you can't allow spontaneity, creativity, and brainstorming, but you need to own your calendar and be intentional about using your time—not just with regard to how you use your time, but how your time is used.

So please take a look at your calendar and be honest about who's managing it.

Make a Decision Already

We make decisions all day long. Research tells us that the average person makes about 35,000 decisions in a given day—about 20 before we get out of bed in the morning.

So it's no wonder that many people end up feeling exhausted at some point in the day. It's natural to get depleted because we are not biologically designed to make many choices and we also avoid making hard choices.

The amount of effort required to do something influences what we think we see, states a new University College, London study that suggests we're biased toward perceiving anything challenging to be less appealing.

"Our brain tricks us into believing the low-hanging fruit really is the ripest," says Dr. Nobuhiro Hagura, who led the UCL team before moving to NICT in Japan. "We found that not only does the cost to act influence people's behavior, but it even changes what we think we see."

University College London. "Humans are hard-wired to follow the path of least resistance." ScienceDaily. ScienceDaily, 21 February 2017.

<www.sciencedaily.com/releases/2017/02/170221101016.htm>

Of course, technology has made this demonstrably worse because we now have the opportunity to make more decisions (good, bad and truly terrible, Dear God, the Denso Vacuum Shoes, what was I thinking?) than we have ever made.

Maybe you've gone through life assuming you are a decent decision-maker because you do it so much. But it's a lot like breathing. You've been breathing your whole life. So what could you possibly have to learn about becoming better at breathing? It turns out a lot.

In fact there are ten different ways to breathe that can assist with resetting the cacophonous static going on in your head.

10 Breathing Techniques to Try

Pursed lip breathing

Belly breathing

Breath focus

Lion's breath

Alternate nostril breathing

Equal breathing

Resonant breathing

Sitali breath

Deep breathing

Humming bee breath

Source: Ghiya S. (2017). Alternate nostril breathing: a systematic review of clinical trials.   msjonline.org/index.php/ijrms/article/view/3581/3158

Guided meditations. (2017).
uclahealth.org/marc/mindful-meditations

Pursed lip breathing. (2018).
my.clevelandclinic.org/health/articles/9443-pursed-lip-breathing

Relaxation techniques: Breath focus. (2008).
health.harvard.edu/newsletter_article/relaxation_techniques_breath_focus

Streeter CC, et al. (2017). Treatment of major depressive disorder with Iyengar yoga and coherent breathing: A randomized controlled dosing study. DOI:
10.1089/acm.2016.0140

Upadhyay Dhungel K, et al. (2008). Effect of alternate nostril breathing exercise on cardiorespiratory functions.
ncbi.nlm.nih.gov/pubmed/18700626

Now, keep in mind that when I say, "good at it," I don't mean that you're making the right or wrong decision because that can be a matter of perspective. I mean, are you an effective decision maker?

Are you decisive?

Do you stall?

Do you move forward?

When you come across a decision, whether you realize it or not, you go through 25 different ways to respond to this situation. And that's part of the problem. If you were to zoom out a little bit and look at the decisions you make regularly, you might find that there's probably only a handful of actual ways to respond in any given situation.

What do you stand for?
What are your values?
What matters?
What doesn't?
What are your goals?
What are you willing to leave behind?

It may sound like a tall order. I'm a 38 year-old man. I believe that I have only recently acquired some inkling of what my core values are and who I might actually be. The true and rightful wizard behind the curtain of productivity is self-exploration. I can't do it for you, but I'm happy to share my experience. If you see yourself in the telling, it may work for you as well.

Teams R Work

Whether or not you have an actual, definitive team, there are people who work for and with you. That's a team. Even if you're a sole practitioner, solopreneur, or work remotely, you still have a team. The people around you—your family, children, friends, neighbors—are all part of your team.

Totally alone? Just you and Doordash? Well, whether you realize it or not, somebody somewhere is going to buy something from you. And guess what? Your clients and customers are also part of your team.

It's the interactions that constitute a team, not a W2. You present an image, a vision, a mantra, a way of doing things with which they will interact. Your existence is tied to theirs, transactionally, metaphorically, operationally. Talk. Listen. Buy. Sell. Give. Take. Yin. Yang.

And it all goes great until it doesn't.

Enter stress and uncertainty and insecurity and maligning secret group chats in Slack.

Guess who's responsible?

No, not Justin, that old pot-stirrer. He's harmless. And lonely and insecure. No, it's not his fault the esprit de corps is tanking.

It sits squarely on the shoulders of the person in charge.

When I was training our puppy, things went well, until they didn't. And I'd slide in my bare feet on the evidence of things not going so well. The dog trainer told me to go to the bathroom, look squarely in the mirror and say, "Bad owner."

It's the same with running a company, no matter how small. If things aren't going well, if your sales and marketing folks left a pile of poo in Airtable, if no one knows where the hell the most current SOP is for onboarding, if your VA leaves his gig to harvest peyote in Real de Catorce, go into the bathroom and repeat after me: "Bad Founder."

There are two ways that entrepreneurs stress out their teams and dismantle community. One is inconsistency. The other one is mismanagement.

So let's talk about inconsistencies and protecting the entrepreneur's team from the entrepreneur's mind.

For example, the founder goes to some conference (remember going to conferences?) and sees a cool new piece of software.

Filled with a dopamine rush that only three days in Orlando can bring, the boss returns. "Hey team, I'm so pumped. I found this game-changing [fill in the blank], and we're going all in. Let's get it implemented."

Everybody freaks out and drops what they're doing to shift gears. Deadlines get missed. People get panicked, work late, get stressed. Two weeks later, deadlines are missed again, and nobody knows why. The founder has moved on to something else, mistakenly confident that his SaaS monkey wrench is operational.

Now, that scenario creates terror in the team's minds, but remember, your team is everybody. Decisions affect your family, clients, and customers, and ultimately you are seen as unreliable by all of them.

You become the boy who cried wolf."

It becomes impossible for people around you to know if this is a real thing. Will it have longevity? Is it a thing you really, really want to do, or were you temporarily and impetuously excited about it?

One of the best ways to mitigate it is to have a system and a structure for how you process ideas. Ideas are great. They're the lifeblood of your business, and it could not exist or grow without them. But they never emerge in a logical form or fashion.

I know you don't want your style cramped. You don't like restrictions. Sorry dude, if you want to see good ideas take flight, you will need a structure. It can be loose, sure, but at the very least, your team needs to know that when they come to work tomorrow, you haven't turned their world upside down... again.

It makes people feel unsafe, and that's not what good leaders do.

To create consistency and structure, you're going to need what I call "the external brain." It's a place to process all the ideas you have during the day. When you have the time (I do it at around 9 P.M. after the kids are in bed), you sort those ideas.

This method takes into account that inspiration and implementation take place in very different parts of our brains and when you sort the idea, you are apt to be more levelheaded, learn new things, and get relevant information. The tactic allows you to avoid the impulse that happens when you listen to a podcast, get this fantastic idea, immediately jump on the phone with your assistant and say, start doing this thing before you've even heard the end of the episode.

And if you want those brilliant ideas to have legs, it's imperative to build in a way for your team to buy-in. I created a framework called the three W's, and it's the only worksheet that I've ever seen where it's filled out by both the idea generator and the executor. It could be the CEO and COO, one partner, and another partner.

35

Say you have an amazing idea. Life-changing really. You write it down, why it's important and why you want to do it. Then give it to the other person, and they have to fill out the boxes.

Who

Why

When

Who might be somebody on your team who has the bandwidth. But you may need to because you don't have it in-house.

Why is your rationale. Build your case.

When is imperative because while it may be a life-changing, game-changing idea, it might not fit in your Q1 goals. It's your partner's job to push back and offer an alternative to which you can both agree.

To Manage or Lead?

Now, the other aspect of an entrepreneur's wiring that can derail the team is management and its misuse.

No one likes a micromanager. People aren't projects. Most of us learn that after failing to get our high school love to stop getting piercings, change the wiper blades, and apply to college, any college.

Micromanagement can disempower people. Because you're telling people that they don't "got this," and it won't get done without your involvement. You are sending a message that they are neither independent thinkers nor self-sufficient workers. Ew.

Leadership is about empowerment. It's about allowing people to make mistakes and recognize that when they learn and grow, so does the organization.

You may not have a traditional team, but if there's a vendor you email and text 16 times a day to find out where a product is, they're not going to play nice. When you don't have a team, you will look to manage whatever you can in order to regain some sense of control.

It might be something at home with your spouse or your kids. It might be Jack and Molly who always leave their garbage cans at the end of the driveway for days, then leave passive-aggressive notes about their Ring security system noticing that I ran over them last Tuesday when I was backing out of my garage.

Wherever you go, you are a part of something bigger than you and it's vital to listen to the misplaced controlling impulses you create and act accordingly. Empowerment provides opportunities to course correct, because communicating effectively what success looks like establishes trust and respect.

When you recognize that throwing ideas out with no particular structure or method gets paired with micromanaging, it's no wonder your team seems less than enthusiastic. It's a situation you are eminently qualified to improve, and the payoff will help everyone thrive.

But the Jack and Molly situation might be hopeless. I'll continue to return the cans up to their garage and watch my Ring to confirm that it's their dog that's never on a leash. Because in the internal battle between being right or being happy, right usually has a lock. I'm a work in progress. We all are.

The Core Work

It all started with this simple question: "What would you do if you could only work an hour a day?"

Imagine this. You're 20 years old, you're working on a project that you're spending 18 hours a day on, you're young, you're full of energy, and you're working nonstop 18 hours a day. All the while, you're building up debt and not getting things done. Hard-charging, being super productive, and after three years you're diagnosed with a chronic illness that nearly kills you. It takes you from working 18 hours a day to barely struggling to get an hour of work on any given day. What do you do? Most people would probably give up.

Or...

You find a new way of doing things in that one hour that you have.

You discover the value of constraint.

Now, that was me when I got diagnosed with Crohn's disease, and my response to that was creating a brand new system of productivity that would allow me to get a maximum amount done, actually more than I'd ever gotten done before in much less time.

If you ask somebody who works a nine to five job "what would you do?", would you ask if they could only work till four? The answer is easy: skip lunch. But if you ask that same person what would they do if they only had an hour of the day to get that work done, what then?

It requires an entirely different kind of thinking, one that most people are not even aware of, because the question wouldn't be about what would you do, it would be about what you *wouldn't* do. If those things that you wouldn't do still have to get done, who or what is going to do them for you?

The whole idea of working smarter versus harder is particularly relevant here. A restriction on time doesn't necessarily mean you can't be more productive. I've seen so many different situations where people thought that they had no more time to achieve something. But time is rarely the problem. It's about how you use it.

And that's how I came up with the idea for Less Doing and The Replaceable Founder Methodology. The model illustrates what I believe is the most effective way to improve communication, project management, and processes, so that you can enjoy freedom, flexibility, and focus, the result of which is unlocked constraints, unleashed teams, and the opportunity to shepherd an unstoppable business.

First, Unlock Constraints

Unlocking constraints is not merely about removing them because they are holding you and your team back. It's also about increasing them.

Seriously, more constraints?

I know, not what you were expecting. But stay with me. It gets really good.

I believe that every one of us already has all of the potential success, productivity, efficiency, or effectiveness inside of us right now.

It's not a resource upon which we can expand. We can't stop at the gas station and fill our tank with more productivity. Now, we can certainly grow as people and become better, more skilled, and more agile. But ultimately, it all buds and grows from the same life force we all possess.

So what's holding you back? What's holding your company back?

Frequently bosses or managers are obstacles.

Maybe you don't have the right resources.

Sometimes it's that you can't get a minute to focus.

But it's rarely because you don't have the skills or the ability.

To remove those roadblocks, leaders need only set a direction for a company and then do everything they can to get out of the way.

The leaders' only job is to clear a path for the team to get through. Not leap out of the weeds every fifteen minutes asking for an update. Or mow four paths of equal and critical importance simultaneously.

Set up the mile markers and get the hell out of the way.

Parkinson's Law, the description of which first appeared in *The Economist* on November 19, 1955, is C. Northcote Parkinson's idea of the natural tendency for officials to make more work for each other. In other words, work expands to fill the time allowed to complete it.

Generally, if you have an hour to complete a task, you'll take an hour. If you have an hour and 15 minutes, it will take an hour and 15 minutes. And if you have 45 minutes, for the very same task, you'll do it in 45.

What often feels like a lack of time to get something done is, believe it or not, a case of having too much time.

"If you want to get something done, give it to a busy person."

I love that the internet can't decide to whom it should attribute this quote. Ben Franklin? Lucille Ball? I guess it's your choice.

43

There's also a story about a guy who wrote a letter to his father that was 11 pages long. At the very end of the letter, he said, I'm sorry for the length of the letter. If I had had more time, it would have been shorter.

So time is both relevant and relative when it comes to the way we utilize it.

Often, unlocking constraints is not about trying to find more time. Nobody gets more time. It doesn't matter how much money you have, how many connections you have. Nobody gets more time. So if we can't get more and are struggling with what we have now, what if we had to do it with less?

Forcing ourselves to do "it" with less spurns innovation.

My favorite example is MacGyver. No one ever said to him, "Hey, Angus" [that was his first name], go across the street to that Home Depot, grab a shopping cart, pick up whatever you need. Then come back here and blow up this building."

The situation was always like, "Hey, here's a life vest and a box of Wheaties. Blow up the building." He could do it because he lacked resources, which forced innovation.

One more example, I've been a volunteer EMT for almost a decade now. We have loads of essential life saving equipment on the ambulance. And I have a big duffel bag with all sorts of equipment in my truck. I also have an emergency backpack in my family car.

But when I go to the park with my kids, when I drive them to school, or when I go to the store, I always have a small, rigid case in my pocket. It's about the size of two phones put together. And in that little box, I've got about 16 different things that can help save a life in almost any situation.

Now, of course, it's not the same as having the big box. I don't have oxygen. I don't have a defibrillator, but I have all the things that I need to stabilize, even the worst of injuries, and keep things from going south. My favorite tool in the small box is a flattened roll of duct tape because duct tape has about 14 different uses in austere medicine. And it all started with me asking, What if I could only carry a tiny number of items in my pocket?

So what if I told you your business could run successfully on the entrepreneurial equivalent of my small medic's toolbox? It's true. Entrepreneurial austerity is yours for the taking. As an EMT, I would never lie to my patients.

Next, Unleash Your Team

So once we've unlocked our constraints and have adopted an Angus [I'm just gonna keep saying it] MacGyver-based, problem-solving attitude, we can unleash the team.

Remember how I said that everything you need is already inside of you? That you have the ability in you, but there's something that's getting in the way? I mean, it was like two pages ago, so I hope you do. Well, it's the same thing when it comes to unleashing the team.

But the difference here is that the hurdle, the problem, the block is almost always *you*. Bottlenecks are at the top, and it's how most companies operate or don't.

If you're an ineffective decision-maker, that alone will turn you into a bottleneck because somebody needs you to make a decision. If you don't do it effectively, aka quickly, there's a logjam.

If you hold somebody up from getting their work done, there's a significant multiplier effect on how harmful it is to you and your team's productivity.

The other thing that has to be addressed here is the culture of success and failure. As a parent and business owner, I'm sometimes guilty of creating a culture that doesn't allow for failure.

Now, do we want failure as a long-term thing? No, of course not. But every successful entrepreneur talks about how their failures ultimately made them successful.

TOTALLY HUGE SIDENOTE: Again, the internet is taking license with the truth. Quel surpris. I found this cool site, Quote Investigator, to investigate the origins of a quote, so you know you're not spreading fake inspirational news.

I checked out this famous one of Thomas Edison's where he said he didn't fail to make a light bulb the first thousand times. Instead, he figured out a thousand ways not to make a light bulb. The funny thing is it was actually his teammate, Walter Mallory, who said it first. So there's that. The more you know.

Anyway, it's near impossible to have real success without some form of failure. Because even if you achieve it, you either won't recognize it or appreciate it. So it's not as simple as telling the people, "Hey, you're free to make mistakes. No one's going to get in trouble here."

It's way more than that—it's more profound. It's about creating opportunities for them to fail in the first place. In many ways, that's the crux of The Replaceable Founder™ methodology. People need to become replaceable so that they can be replaced *up*, not *out* of the organization. If they don't feel like that next thing is something they can or should do, they will hold onto things. They get stuck, and the business gets stuck too. They also miss out on opportunities, and all this vibe does is disempower your team and ensure that they don't want to take a chance.

More often than not, the thing that makes one business more successful than the other companies around it is the ability to accept and capitalize on risks.

Obviously, non-entrepreneurial teams don't have the same risk profile as an entrepreneurial organization. But it still needs to allow not only for failure but also for the encouragement to learn from those failures.

To me, the only true failure is one from which you do not learn.

Finally, Become Unstoppable

Unstoppable sounds really powerful, and it is, but the critical ingredient is forward movement.

In most situations you encounter, including matters of life and death, it's impossible to guarantee that you'll always make the right decision. But 99% of the time, not making a decision is the worst thing you can do.

Are you somebody who can't move forward, unless it's the best, or unless it's perfect? Well then, you, your team, your company, and all the people who depend on you will suffer due to that inaction.

It doesn't mean that we can't pause and brainstorm and reformulate, but we want to do whatever we can to avoid stagnation. When we unlock those constraints and unleash a team, we've removed bottlenecks. We've removed logjams. Moving forward, even an inch, creates momentum and progress.

A big part of being The Replaceable Founder is *freedom*, which means you don't have to be there, in the office, on all the calls, like some ubiquitous destabilizing force. But if the business screeches to a halt were you to leave the office, the calls, the meetings, then momentum ceases. Not ideal.

Conversely, if you're able to give up your role as the bottleneck, put things in motion, then allow them to keep moving forward, through success and failure, progress is guaranteed. Even if it seems imperceptible at first.

Never stagnate, always stay in motion, never stagnate. Always stay in motion.

Did I make it sound like a train? I meant to do that.

The Four Mindsets

The Replaceable Founder™ framework's goal is to help entrepreneurs achieve an ineffable level of focus, freedom, and flexibility commensurate with the adoption of an Inventor Mindset. In other words, it allows you to define success, then enjoy it.

But we can't put the productivity cart before the horse here. Founders need to do the dirty work of unlocking constraints, unleashing the team, and priming the pump to become an unstoppable force capable of partaking in the three Fs.

So if you skipped the dirty work part, like a diet book that gives you the science and research first, when you only want to know what to eat on Tuesday, go back. Read those sections. We'll happily wait for you right here.

We good? Awesome.

I need to talk about mindsets. Now, I'm averse to a leap into the buzzword hive, but sadly, I've got no synonyms at the ready.

Btw, did you know that no one used the word "mindset" twenty years ago? Like, absolutely no one.

I think that's remarkable.

It wasn't until Stanford University psychologist Carol S. Dweck, Ph.D., wrote "Mindset – The New Psychology Of Success" in 2007 that the word exploded in business language.

Her premise was simple.

"Human endeavor can be dramatically influenced by how we think about our talents and abilities. People with a fixed mindset—those who believe that abilities are fixed—are less likely to flourish than those with a growth mindset—those who believe that abilities can be developed." (Dweck, p. 23)

It's now called Decision Theory or General Systems Theory, depending on where you did your MBA. But mindset boils down to a set of assumptions or methods commonly agreed upon by a group. It's your squad's philosophy of life.

The journey toward becoming a Replaceable Founder incorporates four mindsets.

Cog

Engine

Engineer

Inventor

Any person in a business, including the founder, the custodial staff, the customer service specialists, the marketing team, can operate with one of these mindsets.

Let's do some visualization, which will be challenging if I ask you to close your eyes because you won't be able to read. So don't close your eyes.

Imagine a speed bump.

What does it do?

If it could talk, what would it say?

A speed bump with a *cog* mindset will say, "I'm a speed bump. I slow down cars."

The same speed bump with an *engine* mindset will say, "I'm a traffic control device. I help traffic operate more efficiently."

Great. Now we're getting somewhere.

What about the *engineer* mindset? How would the speed bump look at its work then? It would probably say, "I'm a safety device. I help make people safer, which is a great and noble purpose."

Finally, if that speed bump is of the *inventor* mindset and you asked what it does, it will say, "Well, there's a school about a hundred feet down the road. So I save children's lives. That's what I do." Now that's a mission, a purpose that anybody can get behind.

A few months ago, I was giving a Replaceable Founder workshop. We were doing that whole go-around-the-room thing, asking people what they do and this gentleman in the front row said that he delivers summer dreams. There was a collective, almost baby shower sigh, from the audience.

It turns out he runs a pool maintenance company.

He and everybody who works for him are of the inventor mindset that they deliver summer dreams. People of that mindset will show up on time. They'll miss fewer days of work, and they will work harder because it matters more.

How to Level Up

Some people stay stuck at certain levels. Generally, it's fear and ignorance that keep people at the cog level They can't make the leap from cog to engine because they are afraid the responsibility begins and ends with them. After all, they claim that nobody can do what they do, and if somebody could, they would surely be out of a job. So they stay there, shovel faster and harder, and push their way through.

The cog focuses on the minutiae, the boring, the prescriptive. They're doing the requisite tasks necessary to get the company through the day. In terms of flexibility, they're in a cage. They can't go anywhere because if they do, the business will grind to a halt. And forget the notion of freedom. Cogs are barely able to keep their head above water.

Many founders recoil at the notion of being a cog. I get that. It sounds neither glamorous nor impactful. So the way to cast off the mantle of cog-ness is to acknowledge that you may very well be suffering from terminal uniqueness.

Granted, you might've been unrivaled when you started the business, but at some point, you stopped being as singular as you imagine. No disrespect. I've been there. You started doing the work of cogs because it had to be done. There are other people and tons of automations that can do cog work. So maybe ask yourself, Why are you doing it? Because anyone, even you, can jump that line and become the engine.

Now you're the driving force in the business. You are not a part of the engine. You are the engine. You still have to be there, wherever there is, so freedom at this point is elusive. You can't go very far without the business halting, and your focus is firmly on the organization's work. But, you've got enough headspace now to get interested in other work, ideas, projects, pursuits. But you can't because you are otherwise occupied.

But possibilities are the fuel that propels you to go from engine to engineer. Here is where you'll discover the difference between working in the business and working on the business. Your hands-on engagement gives way to the cultivation of ideas. It's more about using your voice instead of your hands. Maybe you go back and forth. Perhaps you spend more time brainstorming, but projects get done whether you are physically there or not.

Engineers focus on challenging scenarios and accelerate meaningful growth. You see some real possibilities in terms of freedom and flexibility. You can self-identify as free-range. Mostly. There are still limits. But many people happily roost here. They hit what I call the "good enough" line. There's freedom. Check. Focus? Check. As long as there's some flexibility it's perceived as good enough. But the problem is that good enough is a trap.

Now don't get me wrong. This isn't some Gordon Gecko, hungry hungry hippo baloney. It's about your mental enrichment, which, come on, will slowly atrophy if left alone. And good enough is probably not good enough for your competitors. When you accept that reality, it's simple to jump the line to inventor.

The inventor gets to focus on their genius, the things that bring them the greatest joy and have the most impact. They have the flexibility to work anywhere, anyhow, anytime.

(I'm writing this during an NYC snowstorm between EMT calls for the Central Park Medical Unit.)

Finally, let's talk about freedom because it's essential.

The Liberty Paradox describes two types of freedom: freedom from and freedom to. When most people talk about freedom, it's something they're trying to escape. The nine to five, the debt, the bad boss, the wrong team, whatever it might be, it's freedom from.

Ultimately what I want for all Replaceable Founders is to have the freedom to explore and then return to the business when you want, if you want, and make the company even better.

I don't want you to leave, but I want you to be able to. Because if you can, it means you have systems, processes, automation, and a team that can grow the business far beyond anything that you possibly could.

Ready to go over my roadmap for the journey?

Best to get your hands off the steering wheel then. Just call shotgun. I got this.

The Levers of Success

The three levers that trigger The Replaceable Founder™ productivity machine are:

Communicate effectively

Manage projects

Perfect processes

When a person can engage the levers at the right time, in the right order, and for the right reason, the transformation is remarkable.

Effective Communication

I start with the notion of communicating effectively for one simple reason. If you can't express yourself well, nothing gets done the way you intend. And I mean anywhere. At work. At home. At the Sonic drive-thru.

I've worked with thousands of individuals over the last decade and hundreds of different companies. I'm confident that 80% or more of the productivity problems in a business that hinder its growth come back to communication—the lack of it, its quality, and its complexity.

I'm not talking about the words you use. That's important and has a place. But there are plenty of people with more expertise than me who can teach about the right words to use. I'm more interested (and qualified) in laying out a communication framework that illustrates what the founder needs to do, what the team needs to do, and where those two roles intersect and integrate.

It begins with the founder limiting him or herself to three decisions. Next, it's imperative to embrace asynchronous communication with your team, your clients, and, well, really anyone with whom you need to have productive conversations.

After those two triggers are firing correctly, it's time to attack the six levels of delegation, where everyone is working in concert with one another to empower the team and untangle the founder.

The Three Decisions

The three decisions belong to you. It's about you, nobody else, not the team, not some piece of technology. It is about you being a resolute, unhesitating decision-maker. And by the way, it doesn't mean that you're always making the right decision. There may not be a right decision in certain situations. But I can tell you something for sure: no decision is almost always the wrong decision.

Every one of you makes a thousand or more decisions on any given day. You assume you're good at it because you've been making decisions your whole life, but 99% of us don't use a framework for making those decisions. So when it comes to important decisions, we don't have anything to fall back on. We don't have any internal compass. If you dig deep and look at your daily choices, I would bet you spend more time on the small decisions than you do on the big ones. The definition of unproductive right there.

For example, did anybody who is married or has children devote months to developing a list of pros and cons of marrying a particular person or having kids before going ahead with either (or both)?

Conversely, how many of you sit on the couch for 10 to 15 minutes choosing the right thing to watch on Netflix?

Big, small, impetuous, measured. Decisions without a framework can get muddled.

One of the coolest frameworks I've discovered is from Herodotus, the Persian philosopher, speaking about the Greeks.

"They are very fond of wine, and drink it in large quantities. To vomit or obey natural calls in the presence of another is forbidden among them. Such are their customs in these matters.

It is also their general practice to deliberate upon affairs of weight when they are drunk; and then on the morrow, when they are sober, the decision to which they came the night before is put before them by the master of the house in which it was made; and if it is then approved of, they act on it; if not, they set it aside. Sometimes, however, they are sober at their first deliberation, but in this case they always reconsider the matter under the influence of wine."

Herodotus: On The Customs of the Persians. Ancient History Encyclopedia. Retrieved from https://www.ancient.eu/article/149/)

However, before building a framework, it's valuable to reflect upon how and why the brain decides. Remember, we all have hard-wired perceptions involved in decisions, but they might not be accurate.

"I'd love to give you an answer, but I have to run it past my partner first."

--*Do I have autonomy, confidence, equanimity?*

"We're not going to your mother's for Thanksgiving."

--*Is this fearful or protective?*

"Let me mindmap that idea first."

--*Am I overthinking or being analytical?*

"Sure, Vegas sounds fun."

--*Is this reckless or adventurous?*

It's not just the type of decision, but also acknowledging that there are certain times when you should be making big decisions and specific times when you should refrain. "Add to cart" after a particularly trying day and its trusty sidekick, "We think you left something behind," spring to mind.

Still, some people have the luxury of and acuity for listening to two different trains of thought about the same decision simultaneously, and that's amazing.

You can hone this skill, and I'll show you how when we get to our discussion of The External Brain (which isn't nearly as gross as it sounds). Not to digress even further, but it's all about adopting one frame of mind for capturing ideas and another for acting upon them.

So finally, back to the three decisions. My enthusiasm for my methodology derails me sometimes. I'm aware of it—first step.

The initial encounter you have with any decision requires only three decisions. It's fascinating that most people end up going through 20, 30, 40, a hundred iterations of any decision. If they sat back for a minute and looked at the decisions they ultimately chose, there will only be about three to five possible and realistic outcomes.

Obviously, there's a difference between, "Do you like the red paint or the blue paint?" and "Which of these 15 logos do you like?" The former is binary; the latter is a more complicated decision. It has detail. I'm talking about the first time you are presented with the opportunity to decide anything. In that situation, I want you to think that you have three choices and only three.

Delete. Deal with it. Defer.

When I came up with this framework initially, clients used it to achieve inbox zero, and it is as valid today as it was ten years ago. But ultimately, it became a framework for decision-making in general. Email was such a great launchpad because it is one of the only opportunities you have in any given day to make hundreds, maybe thousands of decisions.

Human beings are good for about 24 decisions in a given day. Most of you made all of them before you got out of bed this morning, especially if you're on a dating app.

So the first D is **delete**. Remember, again, this was about email originally, but delete can be replaced with decline or deny. Just say no.

Yes got you to where you are, but no will get you where you need to go.

It's easy to say yes—and to make it your future self's problem. It's harder to some extent to say no, unless you stand up for yourself. Say I'm going to say no if it isn't the right opportunity for me, or it's not the right time, or it doesn't ultimately serve my mission. It's not necessary to be a jerk about it. A friend told me she been practicing saying no by saying, "It's more than I can do." And no one can debate that.

The second decision is **deal with it**, and that means deal with it *right now*.

If you can do this, you'll be insulating yourself against an awful, self-sabotaging, self-defeating mindset. The person who can deal with something right now but decides not to deal with it right now is the person who says things like:

"I'll work on it later."

"Oh, it'll only take me a minute. I'll deal with it then."

"OK, just put it on top of the pile. I'll get to it."

I don't know what world we grew up in that we believed our future self is not our actual present self, and that we are going to somehow magically transform into another more productive, head down, git-'er-done being entirely at some later date—not going to happen.

And what is this magical land you all live in where later in the day, there's a time where nobody's bothering you, and you're fresh and motivated and can deal with the work? Certainly not in my house at five o'clock at night when everyone is either hungry, tired, chatty, or just done.

There is no perfect later.

Later is ambiguous.

Later is procrastination.

Later is fear.

If you can deal with something right now, and I mean in the next two to three minutes, and it's not going to require a massive mental shift, then deal with it right now. Not only will you get the tremendous dopamine hit of realizing that you accomplished something, but more importantly, you will avoid something that many leaders, managers, supervisors are guilty of and is an incredibly insidious, selfish, and destructive behavior.

Do you know what it is?

You are holding other people up. If somebody needs you to do something like make a decision, and you say, "I will deal with it later," even if it's an hour, you are preventing that person from doing their work (which, btw, will probably hold someone else up too).

So you're not allowed to be shocked two weeks later when a deadline gets missed. Rather than doing the equivalent of burying one's head in the sand, it's the founder's responsibility to feed everybody else. If you persist in this leadership charade, shame on you. There I said it.

Now **Deal with it** could include delegating. It's a vital subset of this decision.

When you give somebody all of the information and resources they need to get the job done, you're conveying what success looks like. Then you can **deal with it** very quickly. At that moment, you are done. You have accomplished everything that you could. There was nothing else for you to do until that person returns with the work completed. But time is of the essence. If you can't delegate quickly and efficiently, you'll get waylaid.

To me, the third D, **Defer**, is the most fascinating. Now I didn't say procrastinate, which is a fear-based activity. I said defer, which is an owner activity.

If you can't say no, because it has to get done and you can't deal with it right now, including delegating it, then you need to defer it to a time when you can more effectively make that decision.

Remember the drunk/sober Herodotus framework? That's this.

Incorporating the concept of peak time here is invaluable. Do you know about Peak Time, the 90 minutes of the day where you're two to 100 times more effective than any other time of the day? The naturally heightened state of awareness that I built an app for to help you identify?

Once you determine what that is (the app's available on Google Play and the Apple store; don't install it now because this chapter is almost over). It also helps you determine when you are absolutely not effective. For example, I have trouble doing creative work before seven o'clock at night. I'm not great on the phone before noon. Do your best to own your schedule and own your time and defer the right activities to the right times.

In the end, it's not "I'll get to it tomorrow." It's "I will handle this at 10 A.M. on Thursday." Then put it in your calendar. Use a tool to remind you. Tell an assistant to remind you.

But most importantly, get it out of your site. If it's an email, snooze it, if it's a person making a request, ask them to come back at a specific time. Practice out of sight, out of mind. You're signaling to everyone around you that you are constructing a way to make better, more effective decisions, hopefully, more helpful decisions.

I used to work in construction. And I would always tell contractors and subcontractors, "I don't care if this job's going to take three times longer than I want it to take. I want you to be accurate. So don't tell me it's going to take two days. And then it ends up taking five days. Tell me it's going to take five days. I can grumble about it if I want right now. But if you stick to that time, then I can plan accordingly."

69

If you stick with the 3Ds framework, I can assure you that distraction will become another irritating habit you can release. If somebody comes to you with a big or small decision, pick one of three choices and go back to what you were doing.

And bonus! You'll have developed a reputation for consistency. People will know that when you say I will handle this at 10:00 A.M. on Thursday, it will happen. And who doesn't want to be that guy?

Response-Ability

--A look at Asynchronous Communication

The best way to describe the benefit of asynchronous communication is to give you a little scenario that depicts its absence. In the end, I'll type "and scene" because I've always wanted to do that.

Tyler needs to set up the quarterly meeting with the heads of Marketing, Sales, and Customer satisfaction—so four people in total. Since everyone is now working virtually, he must do it on Zoom. He telephones each of the three department heads personally to coordinate. A small but meaningful touch, Tyler thinks.

He optimistically asks each person, "Tuesday, Wednesday, or Thursday? Whatever suits you guys best."

Oh, Tyler, says the omniscient narrator. Your optimism is laudable but so tragically misdirected. Why, why do you do these things to yourself?

And we're off.

Marketing can't do Tuesday, but Wednesday is good.

Sales says Wednesday or Thursday works.

Ditto from Customer Satisfaction.

Wednesday it is. That was easy, Tyler thinks.

He sends out an email to all parties confirming the details.

Customer Satisfaction hits reply all.

Tyler sighs.

Turns out Customer Satisfaction can't do Wednesday but is really, really sorry for inconveniencing everyone. Just go on and have the meeting without her, and she'll watch the recording of the Zoom meeting (she won't).

The conversation now devolves into an emotionally intelligent dumpster fire. All department heads console, endorse, confirm, and celebrate Customer Satisfaction as an integral part of the decision-making process and, in the old days, a valued team member who always brought the very best cronuts.

It's Friday. There is still no meeting scheduled. Tyler decides to postpone it until Q2 when things are back to normal.

And scene.

The second accelerator under the lever of Communicating Effectively is Response-Ability, aka asynchronous communication. It is the single most powerful concept a person can embrace if he (I'm talking to you, Tyler) wants to be more effective.

It is the opposite of synchronous communication, which is a form of call and response—on the phone, on a video chat, sitting face-to-face. Someone speaks, someone responds with an

72

expression, a comment, a question. And it can go back and forth like that for as long as you want (or don't want).

Texts, email, and voice messaging apps are all asynchronous. Even a letter in the mail is asynchronous. At its heart, asynchronous communication works best because you communicate when and how you want.

In an asynchronous communication setting, I can send a message to somebody in my chosen format. They can receive it whenever they choose—to listen to it, read it, take it in, think about it and respond when they want.

I listen to their response when I want to and then back and forth and back and forth. Now, this may sound inefficient or slow to some people, but it works more economically because you're allowing people to communicate when and where they are at their best. You rarely get that in a synchronous setting, even if there are cronuts.

People have different circadian rhythms, live in various time zones, and have any number of momentary disturbances that affect their ability to show up in the moment. I know you're going to say that the best communicators can be fully present on the fly. True, but they are the exception, not the rule. We mere mortals have not honed that skill nearly as well as a political candidate or barefoot CEO.

Face-to-face or screen-to-screen meetings really should be an absolute last resort and should be avoided at all costs. The idea that you could get multiple people on the same page, in the same headspace, at their best, at the same time is misaligned and misguided.

It's one of the reasons that the 9:00 A.M. Monday morning team update meetings usually result in more than one person saying, "Couldn't this have been an email?"—which is mildly passive-aggressive but true nonetheless. Somebody is yawning, somebody is checking Instagram (we see you, Claudia), and someone hasn't yet downshifted from a Sunday eSports vibe.

The collective dissonance has ripple effects that create inefficiencies throughout the day, the week and messes with the company rhythm. Honestly, you could completely tank somebody's day by forcing them to have a meeting at the wrong time. Granted, sometimes it's unavoidable, but avoid it when you can.

When you communicate asynchronously with someone else, sure, it might take longer, but ultimately you're going to get a better result. Hands down, a better result.

I do all my private coaching asynchronously using a voice communication app. I exchange voice messages with my clients regularly and have clients who send me three, four, five messages a day. Sometimes they might be for a minute or two. Occasionally they'll send me a much longer message when they need to vent.

When somebody sends me a juicy, meaty problem, I can think about it. I can research it, and if I need to, I can talk to another expert about it, all before responding.

Whether I get back to that person in 10 minutes or two days, I'm going to come back to them with an answer that solves their problem. It might sound grandiose, but imagine if every issue presented to you was done in a way that allowed you to solve it in your own time with all the resources you needed to accomplish it?

It's more powerful than a traditional client check-in where all the week's issues have to be memorialized somewhere and ticked off in some random order. It never works, and it winds up being like that book club we all joined where all anyone talked about was why they didn't have time to read the book.

Ineffective communication is due in part to the misuse of asynchronous communication tools. Somebody writes a text message to somebody. Then they hold the phone—waiting, watching for the bubbles to pop up. Wrong! It's not the way it's supposed to work. You're supposed to be able to send that message, put down your phone, and go back to doing what you need to be doing. Waiting for a response is a waste of valuable time, and quite honestly, it can make you feel like an awkward teenager, wondering whether she'll go to the prom with you. I'm so not going back there.

We see distracting, interrupting communication a lot in email, chat, and group communication channels. In combination, they can be a real-time suck. Better to get in the mindset that you are using these tools to communicate with yourself or the world. These tools are not meant to be a portal where the outside world can get a hold of you whenever they want.

Here's a challenge for you. Push the limits of what you can accomplish asynchronously:

> Try a team stand-up
>
> Conduct a daily meeting
>
> Make a sales call
>
> Create some content

I do all these things asynchronously. I don't have one phone call on my calendar, not one client meeting, not one group check-in. It isn't necessary. I have taken back control of my time, allowed others to take back control of theirs, and the result is an efficient, thoughtful communication construct that delivers exceptional results.

The Six Levels of Delegation

--Say what you mean, and mean what you say, every time.

Imagine a task you don't want to do or one you are terrible at (or both). You think, "I've got to get this off my plate today." I'm going to stop you right there. Did you know you've already, consciously or unconsciously, decided that the only solution is to give it all to somebody or do it yourself? And neither of those are particularly fantastic choices. When it comes to delegation, many folks think there is no grey area. It's a binary issue. All or nothing. This or that.

If your knee jerks when you think of delegation, the results, I promise, will be underwhelming. If you give away work that is not fleshed out and concise, you will get back non-fleshed out, concise work. Suppose you take something inefficient and give it to somebody else who has fewer contexts and less information—not going to work.

If your delegation process leaves details to the recipient's implicit understanding, frustration will be the only outcome.

Murkiness is not going to work.

We need to make the implicit explicit.

We need to be clear about the parameters, the resources required, and the criteria for success. It's way past time to define the sandbox in which the delegate can play.

Welcome to the third accelerator under the lever of Communicating Effectively.

The Six Levels of Delegation.

The approach posits that there are six gradient levels within which you can delegate to anybody for anything. It's important to note here that it's not that one level is better than another. It's not that level six is better than level one. Instead, it is isolating and then applying what's appropriate for the task, your comfort level, and the delegate's competency.

Level One is: Do what I say. Don't think. Don't give me your opinion. Don't vary. Just do what I'm telling you to do.
Level Two is: Look into this and get back to me. Do some research. Find some options. Then come back to me with what you find. Save me the effort of doing that work.
Level Three is: Give me your advice. Look into this thing and then come back and tell me what you think we should do.

See how we're dialing up the level of empowerment?

Level Four is: Do what you need to do, make a decision, but keep me in the loop.

Level Five is my favorite: Decide within limits. The limit could be money, time, or space. But the most common limit is a dollar amount that you're comfortable within which people can make decisions.

In my company, you don't need to discuss any decision that is $500 or less. The number is subjective according to your comfort level and business. But think about a time when you were unavailable to make a decision. Something didn't move forward because there was a $25 difference in the price of something and someone wasn't sure they had the authority to decide. Imagine how frustrating that must've been and how the fallout from the delay might have caused something potentially significant.

So decide within limits.

Level Six is: Get it done. I don't care who you have to hire or how much it costs. Just make it happen.

Now, level six is a fascinating tipping point. It is not about saying, "I trust you implicitly." After all, it's probably somebody who has some specialty like a coder or a graphic designer or a sales funnel builder.

No, level six is saying you have no involvement in the task you're delegating. You would only hinder the process.

I just spent eight months getting my website overhauled. Of course, I had input on the graphics and wording, but they were the experts. I don't know if this red is better than this red, and I don't care. You choose what's best because I'm paying you and trusting you and your ability.

Create a simple worksheet for yourself that asks and answers the following questions. It will help you delegate tasks more effectively than you ever thought possible.

> What is the task?
>
> When does it need to be done?
>
> What does success look like?
>
> What are the criteria for success?
>
> What are the resources needed?
>
> Only contact me if...

If you ask somebody to buy a plane ticket for you, they need a payment method, identification, or passport. Preempt confusion and conversation.

The last thing on the worksheet is "only call me if." Let's use the plane ticket as an example. If they can't get the window seat, that's not a good enough reason. If they can't get a vegetarian meal, you can pack something. But if they can't get a seat in the first or second row, then I want you to tell me.

Remember, the level is entirely dependent on the task, and any task can be on any level. Again, it depends on your level of comfort, that is, what may or may not be appropriate for the task and the person's perceived competence to whom you're giving it.

Let's say that I want a new customer relationship management system for our business.

Level One would be: "So-and-so sign up for this service."

Level Two would be: "Hey, we need a CRM. Can you look at the best options for us? Come back to me with a few choices, and I'll take it from there."

Level Three is: "Tell me which customer relationship management system you think we should sign up for and why."

Level Four is: "Sign up for a customer relationship management service. Let me know which one you think we should go with. Inform rather than consult."

Level Five is: "We need a CRM. I don't care which one you get. I don't want it to be more than $500 a month. We have 50,000 contacts on our mailing list."

Level Six is: "We need a new CRM. See you. I'll be gone for a few days."

It's fine to name the levels when delegating. While telling someone that it's a Level One task may not be necessarily empowering, it is concise. The same is valid for telling someone it's a Level Six job. They know they are ultimately empowered to take on the responsibility, have the freedom to decide, and accept the consequences (good or bad) of their actions.

Intentions matter here. So the next time you delegate, don't just think about what you're delegating. Think about how you're doing it. If your intentions are clear, you will get back exactly what you intended. And isn't that all any of us really want?

Managing Projects

The Replaceable Founder™ framework's second significant area of focus, or lever, as it's known around here, is Project Management. It means managing myriad tasks that help achieve a goal. Or, to put it rhetorically, project management answers the question, "What needs to get done to get where we want to be?"

It follows Communicating Effectively for a good reason. If one can't master the art of communication with people, wrapping one's head around all the moving parts of a project is impossible. If you skipped to this part of the book, doing that whole TL;DR thing, I see you. I am you. But please, go back to page 34. I'll wait for you here.

Now, let's get started and see if we can build a more productive brain.

The External Brain

If you want to create a well-oiled system for processing your ideas, take a moment and think about:

How many ideas do you get on a given day?

How many do you forget?

Do you fall down a rabbit hole when inspiration hits?

Do your ideas become disruptions? For you? For your team?

How well do your ideas get executed?

Never? Sometimes? Always?

Look, you need a system for processing ideas. Having a notebook or a journal is good, but it's not the same as having an integrated mechanism for processing your thoughts.

So let's break down the ideation of ideas, ideally. (That's some next-level alliteration right there. I've had two cups of coffee. It could go off the rails real soon.)

There are essentially three states of mind when it comes to an idea. First, there's inspiration, which can happen anywhere, anytime. Driving. In the shower. In a meeting, boom. You get a great idea for something.

"Why don't we put together a clearinghouse of resources for our clients, free to people just starting, but put it behind a paywall for folks who have reached a certain level of revenue? OMG, what a fantastic idea. I really need to talk to Jasmine about this. Wait, what? Do I have the Q3 metrics on Social Media engagement? Crap. Focus, Brad, focus."

The brain is excellent at coming up with ideas. It isn't good at holding on to them. The problem that entrepreneurs tend to face is that they'll get a great idea, affirm it to themselves as most definitely a great idea. And because fear of losing the idea grips them, they'll go off down the so-called rabbit hole, mesmerized by the shiny object of their brilliance.

Three hours later, you may realize it's not such a great idea. Worse than that humbling revelation is the cringe-worthy fact that you've already told your team about this fantastic idea, asked them to start working on it, and now you have to go back, contrite and apologetic (not your strong suit) and take it all back.

Let's stop doing that. Here's how:

Idea Capture

The only thing you are responsible for right now is to capture those ideas quickly without judgment. Don't categorize it as a good idea or a bad one. It's just an idea. Get it out of your head. I don't care where.

> You could have a notepad on your desk.
>
> You could tell it to a smart home device, then create a reminder for the device to play your ideas back to you at a specific time.
>
> You could send yourself an email.
>
> You could record a voicemail to yourself
>
> You can even have a waterproof Post-it note pad in your shower (my favorite).

And do it quickly. You never want to take more than 20 seconds to capture an idea. Honestly, many of them will be garbage, but would you rather hold on to that idea, renting space in your head? Get it out so you can examine it later when you might do something with it.

Next, pick a time to sort those ideas. It could be hours or even days after the ideation itself. The tool you use doesn't matter. It's entirely up to you. It can come to you as an email digest, which you can set up as an automation through IFTTT or Zapier, timeless evergreen platforms.

Sidebar: I try my best not to denote specific tools because, well, things change, and people are different. Also, I have no affiliate relationship with any of the tools I do happen to mention because that's gross.

If you don't want to automate it, collect your bits of paper in a bin on your desk.

I do my sorting as part of a nightly routine. I go onto Trello, where I store my ideas.

Oh, this is something that I wanted to talk to my COO about. So I'm going to assign it to her and make a comment.

This is something I wanted to buy. So I'm going to purchase it, or I'll send it to a VA to buy.

This is something I needed to tell my wife about. So I'm going to talk to her about it right now.

The Three Ws

The significant and enduring ideas require a specific method I like to call The Three Ws.

Maybe you had an idea at two in the afternoon. It's now eight o'clock at night, and the idea still looks good. You want to talk to the team about implementation. First, you have to put it into a format that demonstrates that the concept is fleshed out, so it doesn't feel like you're dumping more stuff on somebody.

I sense some resistance.

I understand that what I'm suggesting sounds like I'm slowing down your idea flow, cramping your style, and dampening your creativity. But hear me out. Your ideas will come to fruition more if you have a structure for them in the long run.

I'm not asking you to throw away ideas. I'm asking you to pump the brakes.

Okay, so The Three 3 Ws go like this: There are six boxes on the page, and it starts with:

What is the idea? And why you think it's interesting or important.

Your part is done. You've said your peace. You've made your case.

Now hand it off to whomever is going to execute it for you or with you. If you are a solopreneur with no team, you can still do this. Put it away, then revisit it in a day or two.

First, answer the question: Who needs to do this? It may not be a person you have on your team. It may not be a person at all. It may just be a set of skills that are needed to complete this task. So let's say it's a graphic designer. Okay, well, we don't have one on the team. So that's not someone on the team. We need to hire someone with a particular set of skills (no, not Liam Neeson).

Next, Why? Well, we don't have this skill set in-house, and we need these particular skill sets. If you have someone in-house, you still might say, we need somebody else because that person doesn't have the bandwidth.

When? We need to jump on this right now. Why? Because it's a fantastic idea, Conversely, it can go like this. It's a great idea, but it doesn't fit with our current focus of this quarter, so let's make it a Q3 project.

Now all decision-makers have had a chance to weigh in on the idea. It has a timeline and a responsible person attached to it. This the logical and efficient external brain mechanism at work: capturing ideas into a system that separates the crap from the gold, then employs an inclusive process for actually getting them done.

Radical Transparency

Where everyone knows everything and no one wonders why.

It's a secret wish of mine to install my four-year-old daughter's voice in every company's project management system.

Here's how I imagine it playing out.

You dutifully make a card in Trello that says, "First Quarter Marketing Strategy Session with all Stakeholders."

You hit return, and my daughter says, "Why?"

"Because we have to," you answer.

"Why?" She queries once again.

"Because everyone has to help develop an actionable strategy, that's why," you say emphatically.

So, you assign the card to everyone who needs to be at the strategy session. Hit return, thinking that'll stop her. Oh no, my friend, you do not know my daughter.

"Why?" She says again, this time with a bit more Paw Patrol Cred.

"Because marketing is the key to our ability to scale and if we don't nail down a strategy, instead of just throwing spaghetti up against the wall and seeing what sticks, our numbers are going to tank and I'll be out of a job."

"You can throw spaghetti at your job? Why?"

Now, this can and will go on for the time it takes to get to karate lessons or until your project management system has Radical Transparency. Your choice, but let me warn you, she's indefatigable and unrelenting.

To-Do, Doing, Done

Yes, we all want to get things done. We want projects to proceed systematically, but that's not good enough. There needs to be an understanding of why we use a project management tool, system, or framework at all.

I think it's so everybody can access what's going on at any given time, not get a notification for every adjustment or update. The entire project is laid out in one place, so anyone involved from top to bottom can get a look at what's happening,

Levels of involvement vary when it comes to project management, depending on your corporate culture. Some founders are in the weeds daily, some completely and blissfully unaware of the progress of most projects. Both are unworkable approaches.

On one end of the spectrum is micromanagement, and on the other end, we have a form of emancipation, the freedom to take risks and complete tasks without oversight. Radical Transparency can act as a bridge between those two extremes. Whatever system your company decides to use, the tool doesn't matter, but the architecture does. For me, that is the Kanban method.

Now, business lore says the idea was born on Toyota's factory floor. But the system originates from a stock replenishment system developed in British factories producing Spitfires during World War II. They used the "two-bin system" or a series of empty boxes to signal the need for part replenishment.

Toyota picked up on the idea in the late forties studying supermarkets and brought it to their automotive factories.

Assembly lines and moving through phases logically go against how our brain's wiring, making the system so valuable. It forces us to look at work from a decidedly different perspective. It is **not** a To-Do list.

Kanban's features are:

    The workflow has logical steps.

    Phases are dividing into To Do, Doing, Done

    Work is pushed into the board and pulled through it.

    Bottlenecks are easily identified.

Again, it doesn't matter what tool you use. It matters that the system has a sense of dynamism. Post-it notes on a whiteboard work beautifully, as long as you can move things around.

Every task needs to have one owner, a sole proprietor. It doesn't matter if multiple people are working on it, but that's not the same as an owner or person you can go to if things are not on track. Because if something goes wrong (and it always does) and no one owns it, then no one owns the problem or the solution.

Each card also needs to have a due date on it. Now the due date is instructive because it's not necessarily a hard deadline, but a time for a significant and comprehensive update.

For example, ACME Probiotic Desk Chairs is my company. I'm the project leader on everything. I asked Sarah every other day, "Hey, what's happening with the website build?" She'll invariably say, "Oh, nothing. It's all on track" (which isn't what I asked and seems vague and quite frankly makes me nervous). "But where are we with the graphics? Who should I talk to?" Sarah will say, "I've got it covered, don't worry" (which, again, is not a robust update and does nothing to quell my lingering feeling of dread).

Still, I don't want to micromanage. If a board had all the components of the website built with individual cards for individual tasks with an owner assigned to each, I wouldn't have to bother Sarah or question her oversight.

I could see things moving. I could see bottlenecks. I could address specific questions. I could calm the heck down. That's Radical Transparency. It's not designed to get people "in trouble." We're not in middle school. No adult should ever feel like they are "in trouble." Radical Transparency creates a fantastic opportunity for people to offer help to somebody without them having to ask for it.

It doesn't take a psychologist to know that it's a lot easier to accept help than to ask for it. It's the maximal thing you can do as a leader: offer assistance. You can do it seamlessly by creating Radical Transparency. If you can, Sarah will never say, "Oh, I know, I tried to get it done. I thought I could, and I buckled down, but it didn't work out."

Instead, you will be able to see exactly where and with whom a project has hit a roadblock. You can then reach out and say, "Hey, Sarah. I've got some bandwidth today. How can I help?"

How's that for a radical shift in perspective?

Account-Ability

The breeding ground for responsibility and empowerment.

One of the benefits of creating a system that provides radical transparency is holding people to account for their work. Again, not middle school. No one is going to hear their name on the announcements intercom after homeroom. It is not about finding fault.

Accountability breeds responsibility. It breeds empowerment.

Quick Accountability Sidebar...

One of my clients asked me about project managers. He said he gets ideas all the time just as an entrepreneur does. He was looking for someone who can take those ideas and run with them and get it done. He wants to do the fun part and then hire someone to make it happen.

"So, is that a project manager?" He asked me.

"Well, it could be," I told him.

I prefer to look for certain qualities a person possesses, rather than a LinkedIn-worthy searchable title. There are two attributes I seek out when somebody is going to work with me regularly: attention to detail and initiative.

I don't believe these qualities are trainable. It's an innate ability to take that extra step without having to be told and once there tick all the boxes. I have invariably found these qualities in women who have served in the Armed Forces. I don't think the military instills those qualities necessarily. I think it's something about the type of woman who is drawn to military service and therefore excels in it.

So what is that role, that project-managing, problem solving, detail-oriented position?

I call it a Fixer.

Here's some context. I consider myself to be extremely resourceful. I've always been able to take care of myself. You could drop me in the middle of a country I'd never been to, and I would do fine. But as an entrepreneur, when I get a new idea, it's exciting, and although I'm raring to go my impatience gets in the way. Why? It's because I'm not an attention-to-detail guy.

It's a problem that you need to solve. It's an itch that you have to scratch. It's a curse and a blessing, but that's the definition of entrepreneurship. We come up with some of the most innovative ideas ever, but then we have to do something about it. So it would help if you had somebody who can fix it, line it up, move it along, bring it to fruition.

But not in a *Pulp Fiction* or *Ray Donovan* way. I'm not talking about hiding a body. I'm talking about solving the problem.

There's a Yiddish word: *macher*. It means someone who gets things done. Ultimately, it's what every one of you probably needs, maybe not now, but at some point. So when you're scratching your head, saying, "I need a VA who can do these things, I need a project manager, I need an operations director," you may indeed need those things, but what you probably really need is a fixer: a solver of complicated and disjointed problems.

When I used to work in construction, my nickname was Tylenol because I got rid of headaches. I didn't always know how to make it happen, but I figured it out. We all come up against a wall at times. Figuring out a way around it, through it, or over it is the job of a fixer. If you need one, hire for these specific skills:

Extremely resourceful

Takes the initiative

Preoccupied with the details

Possesses an incredible sense of self-efficacy

Knows "it" can get done

May not know how but will absolutely figure it out

The person laying out the mission doesn't need to know the details. They don't need to know what it takes or even have to think it through. They want a result. And the fixer provides that result.

A fixer installed at the helm of any project is a foundation for success.

But more important than the fixer is a system of accountability that flows through your organization. If it's done the right way, your team will know who they're accountable to and responsible for. (There was no way to write this sentence without using a preposition at the end, without sounding Shakespearean. Apologies.)

They know they own the work. Yes, things will go wrong, and a healthy business creates space for people to make mistakes without nasty retribution or consequence. The only failure is a mistake that we don't learn from. (Again with the preposition. Curses!)

It may be time to create a system for parts of your business you have not previously brought systems to or didn't think you needed because the work was easy and obvious to you.

Accountability might sound like something you don't need a system for because, "Hey, I got something wrong. I'm going to own up to it. I'm going to say that I got it wrong. And you know, everybody will be happy about that. And we'll learn from it."

It's not good enough.

The system that you need is a simple one. It's been around for a long time. It's called The Five Whys, and it's a systematic, structured way of breaking down and finding a solution to a problem.

First, you identify the problem.

Then you answer, why did that happen?

Then answer again.

And so on.

It's akin to interrogation but without the presumption of guilt, bad coffee, or harsh lighting.

For example:

Why do the workbooks for the conference look so lousy?
We missed the deadline at the good printer.
Why?
Because we couldn't agree on a cover.
Why?
Because Josh and Kit argued for two weeks over it.
Why?

Because Kit feels belittled by Josh and Josh just needs to be right.

Why?

Because Josh is really intimidated by her and so he treats her like a secretary from Mad Men.

What makes this exercise powerful is that it provides employees and team members with tools to solve their problems. So they can go to their supervisor or other teammates with a clear identification of the problem and an overt suggestion for a solution.

You can and should also do this exercise when something you do doesn't go according to plan. If you do it *before* drama ensues, or a client goes ballistic, it's a proactive and concrete way to up your game.

Often it's something much more straightforward than you might have thought initially.

Often it's something you probably never thought of, to begin with.

Often you can reverse engineer the set of dominoes that led to this problem. Eliminate that first domino (Josh), and it won't happen again.

Real talk: If you don't have a system in place for people to take ownership, embrace accountability and responsibility, and solve their own problems, their problems will become your problems.

Perfect Processes

In the Replaceable Founder™ system, the final lever is Perfect Processes. The name itself is not an adjective, noun coupling; it's a transitive verb, direct object vibe. The methodology teaches you how to get to perfection. It hasn't already arrived. *For more breathtaking insights into the difference between transitive and intransitive verbs, when to use, and other confounding English language complexities, check out*

https://academicguides.waldenu.edu/writingcenter/grammar/verbs.

Okay, back to productivity.

Perfecting processes comes after you've done the work of getting your communications in order and your project management on track. While it might be tempting for some people to start by making a cool, automated, optimized process upfront, that's not the best use of your time or resources.

You're better off putting good communications in place because good communication will not trump a lousy process, but it will help you overcome a bad process much more quickly. Oh, and it will probably help identify a process that isn't optimized a lot faster. So please resist the urge to skip ahead. You could go through communications and product management overhauls quickly (a matter of days) if you focus on it.

We can always become more efficient. We can take advantage of new technologies and outsource to providers who can integrate into those platforms. So perfecting those processes is a long journey, and quite honestly, there is no destination. Technological advances are making sure of it.

Many people think that this type of efficiency is unnecessary and dehumanizing. They believe they simply need to train people better. I call BS on that. Training isn't going to make bad processes good. You need to make better processes because the better the process, the less training you need.

I had a client with a 182-step process that no one thought could be replicated or mastered by someone without any training. They were wrong.

Now of course, you must train people in soft skills, like how to greet a customer, but for SOPs and processes, they should be able to follow a checklist and learn the process.

There's a difference between learning and training. I'm a fan of learning. I think training is somewhat antiquated.

Commit to a thorough "How we do things around here" house-cleaning. I guarantee it'll be a worthwhile exercise in lasting productivity.

Optimize For Clarity

The way you do the things you do

The framework I developed over ten years ago started with three simple directives needed to achieve real productivity. The Less Doing mantra, Optimize, Automate, and Outsource—and in that order for a good reason. No skipping around allowed, or the results will be meh.

The first step is to identify what you've got now. It might sound simple and obvious, but so many companies don't do a thorough inventory and ask themselves:

Why do we do it this way?

Sometimes, people go through the motions, entrenched in the notion that well, "We've always done it this way." The death knell of innovation right there. Because while you're doing things, the way that it's always been done, some other company, some other person is innovating and doing it better and outperforming you. I know that realization stings a bit. But like a good sting, a helpful sting, a sting that will propel you forward.

So when breaking down a process, it's not only about the steps involved. It's also about tracking the time dedicated and the money spent on our working day's various parts.

How many hours do people spend on email?

How long are team meetings?

How much money is allocated to fixing problems?

What's the turn-around time for a customer inquiry?

We can track all the above and get rich, easy-to-interpret data. In many cases, people operate in a self-imposed vacuum, ignoring the solutions to their problems. The last thing they want to do is stop and look at just how bad it is. But finding out what's going on without assigning blame is the only way out of inefficiency and discord.

It's time to pick a process, any process that is repetitive in your business.

Do you have it documented?

Do you know where it is?

When was the last time it was updated?

Who tested it recently?

Next, how do you teach others this process?

Did the person most familiar with the process put together a comprehensive manual?

Sorry, bad idea. Invariably, it's expertly written but impossible to follow. There's probably zero transferability and a lot of unconscious holes in the documentation. This person has developed natural and instinctive shortcuts they don't even realize they have.

There's an urban legend about Martha Stewart. Lore has it that she always left out a critical ingredient when sharing the recipes for her magnificent baked goods. Originally, she got a bad rap for doing it on purpose so her audience felt inadequate, but really it was simply that the woman knew how to make scones in her sleep, and neglected to impart the secrets of baking soda and boiling water.

Alternatively, do you show somebody how to do it?

Maybe it's a screencast of a digital process on your computer, or you physically show somebody how to do something. Then direct the person to do it. It's the same problem. The student will mirror the teacher's mistakes, inefficiencies, and shortcuts, with context or a baseline to course correct.

So in both teaching methods, people will make mistakes, and when people find a process difficult or frustrating, or they know that there's something wrong with it, they stop using it.

The right way to tackle this is something I call POS. No, not that POS. I'm not talking about PCs. It stands for Process

Optimization System, where we flip Standard Operating Procedure on its head. Here's how you can do it at home:

> Introduce the process. "I'm going to show you what it is. And now you write down the checklist, you write down the steps that you saw and what the process is as you see it. "Now take the checklist and process you've written down, bring it to another person and ask them to run through the checklist and complete the process.
> "It won't work, and that's great!"

Here's how it will probably go:

The third person will go through the process. On step two, where it says, "Open the November document," that person will look at it and say, "Where is that document? How do I access it?"

Here is where you must identify assets in absolute terms.

Instead of saying, "the document from November," put in a link and say, "To open this document, click the link. If you need a password, it's in your password manager under this category."

Now they get down to step seven, and it says, "Once you're finished with this, go to the tab marked 'engineering' and load the document there." They say, "I don't see a tab that says 'engineering'."

So now you have to look at that and say, "Oh right, because I'm logged in as an admin, or I'm logged in as an engineer, and you're not because you're a guest."

Now we get to the final step. "Once you finished with everything, send an email to Roger in accounting and let them know it's complete. The person thinks, "Roger hasn't worked here in three months."

Here is where it's critical to refer to people in a relative sense.

It's not Roger; it's "Account Manager." It's still dynamic information, and it's not pinned to a person, but it allows the person to identify where the data is to go accurately.

Now you might have a five-step process that takes you a few minutes to fix. You might have a 182-step process, and it could take a month to get to this point. But once you do, once you figure out all the holes, the redundant steps, and inefficiencies, you end up with a process that can be accomplished by somebody at a tertiary, not just secondary level. It means you could grab somebody off the street, and they can go through this process without any error.

Congratulations!

You've set up an almost perfect process. And not to move the goalposts on you or anything, but it puts you in an ideal position to look at automation and then possibly outsourcing.

But even if you don't take it any further, you now have a bulletproof process that you can store in a place where people can easily access it. There are many tools designed explicitly for this, and they are accessible online. But the mechanism is not really what's important here. The important thing is having a process anyone can master.

Automate for Precision

When this thing happens here, this thing happens over there.

Yes, we're at the automating part of the methodology. It's the long-awaited, let's-get-our-geek-on moment.

Automation can seem tricky to some people, but you're halfway there if you break it down into triggers and actions. Indeed, there are more complex automations, like things that use artificial intelligence and machine learning. And I love talking about those and only stop talking about them when I notice people looking at their phones, picking at their sweaters, or shifting in their chairs. Read the room, Ari. Read the room.

First, what can be automated? The answer is in the word, "every." Listen carefully to yourself and your team on any day that ends in Y. How many times does someone say,

Every time we send out a newsletter...

Every time a customer complains...

Every time a client's contract is up for renewal...

Every time we hire a new salesperson…

Every time someone uses our affiliate link…?

If it's repetitive, it doesn't need you (not that you're not important). If there's something that happens because something happens, it can be automated.

For example, take one of your super-smooth, bulletproof, optimized processes. Get to a step that says something like, "Save the document to Dropbox, then drop spreadsheet into our accounting software." Ding-Ding Ding. Automate it. The trigger is putting the document into Dropbox. The action is that you want the information from that file to be put into your accounting system.

If you asked a hundred people to tell you what's so great about automation (and not your mom; she still won't visit if you're running the Roomba because "It's troubling"), they'll say that the great thing about automation is that it's cheaper than a human. It works all the time. It never takes a day off, never gets sick. It's scalable.

Yes, all those things are right. But automation reduces errors and that's the best part. Sure, mistakes are costly, but what's more insidious is not knowing when or where they happen. Often, the issues that keep entrepreneurs up at night are:

"I hope that billing issue got taken care of."

"I know that we just launched, but did we post it on Instagram as we planned?"

"Did we remember to send that new client the welcome gift?"

"Does Jeremy still have access to the resource library even though his Stripe payment failed—again?"

That "Oh, man. Did that thing get done?" detracts from your ability to be truly effective. When you don't have to worry, when automation has it covered, peace of mind is tangible. The part of your brain that is preoccupied with living in the wreckage of the future can move on to calmer waters.

Now resist the urge to go ham on this automation idea. Don't take some huge, critical process in your business and pick that to automate. Don't hire someone and spend the next two months figuring out that beast.

Please start with the things that take somebody 30 seconds to do, but they're doing it dozens, even hundreds of times a day. Inputting emails. Counting SKUs. Posting to Twitter. Those are the things that you want to automate right now. It's worth spending 10 minutes to automate something that will save 30 seconds because it's going to save 30 seconds over and over and over and over.

Then, it's just a matter of knocking the pins down one by one, automating as much as possible, and if and if and when you find something that can't be automated, ta-da! We have arrived at the last part of the productivity flex: outsourcing.

Outsource For Empowerment

Give it Away. Give it away now.

Outsourcing is the final piece of the puzzle in The Replaceable Founder™ methodology. Guess what? I did that on purpose. Outsourcing first rarely produces the desired result. Sadly, it usually ends up being an epic failure.

I speak from experience. I've outsourced thousands of hours of work, and I've had spectacular experiences and head-scratching, what-was-I-thinking messes. Once you involve a human being, you open yourself up to errors and mistakes, which is natural; I'm not disparaging bi-pedals. We are, after all, the only beings still capable of inspiration and automation will never do that.

You may also put somebody in a position to feel disempowered. And that's not a good look.

Outsourcing goes pear-shaped:

If you give somebody annoying work.

If you outsource something because you're avoiding or disinterested in it.

If you are in a rush and are sure, there's got to be someone on Fiverr.

It's also very likely that a poor attitude about the work will translate directly to the person doing it. It's like when my kids say, "Dad, this mac 'n cheese is awful. Taste it." Not my favorite dad responsibility.

On the other end of the spectrum, maybe you give somebody something exciting and interesting. The best mac 'n cheese ever. You run the risk of them taking ownership and not sharing the mac 'n cheese because it's "theirs."

The processes they use become opaque, transparency disappears, and the person attached to the work becomes a liability. They could leave. They might get sick. They might have a bad day and not do it the way that you could do it. And yes, to err is human. It is all part of culture and teams, but you can avoid these things quite easily (see the previous 75 pages of this book).

Outsourcing and delegating should be seen as interchangeable words, whether you're talking to somebody who works on your team full time or if you're outsourcing to an outside provider. And the decision process has a pretty straightforward outline.

It's called the DONE method, which stands for Delegate, Outsource, Now, Empower. And it looks something like this:

It's also essential to incorporate the notion that there are four quadrants of outsourcing. The first two are a Generalist and a

Specialist. A Generalist is usually an assistant. It could be a virtual assistant, an in-person assistant, an organizational support system, but it's essentially a Jack (or Jill) of all trades. It may very well be the idea of the fixer that I've talked about before.

The Specialist is obvious. It's a graphic designer, coder, copywriter, somebody who has some specialty. Now, you can access either of those in one of two forums: dedicated and on-demand. Dedicated means one person. You always deal with the same person. They get to know you and your habits. You develop a relationship.

The on-demand model indicates that you have a pool of talent from which to grab. That pool might be two people. It might be thousands of people.

I am not a fan of a dedicated model for anything. I don't feel that people should have a dedicated assistant, graphic designer, coder, or copywriter. The attachment is unnecessary because today it's possible to engage transactionally with anyone.

I prefer to work with an on-demand service where I can benefit from many people with different experiences and perspectives and unlimited bandwidth. You never have to worry about somebody being unavailable, as most of these services offer built-in redundancies. They ensure that the other people are aware of the systems and processes you use with any particular individual.

It's a practical constraint that forces you to innovate and optimize and automate more efficiently, so you don't have to explain things over and over again. If you have a rock-solid process, anybody can get involved and do it the way you want.

When I initially created a process for my podcast creation, I designed it to be a different show writer and audio engineer every single time. I pick and choose marketplaces every time, and it works because there's a reliable process to follow.

The purpose of all this non-attachment is self-protection.

If you've optimized your processes, you'll end up benefiting from unlimited bandwidth and usually less expensive providers. You never have to worry about someone leaving and taking with them (not in a negative way) a process they and they alone have mastered.

Finding the right fit is a genuinely personal decision, but everyone should know which tools add value to the mix. You can think about it as a bellows for a fire. You can open and expand and contract and minimize as needed to suit the business as it grows.

The Ultimate KPI

I'm sure you're thinking, I totally get the theory and I can put lots of this to good use, but what I really want to do is keep it going for the rest of my time here on the planet. How do I do that, Mr. Productivity?

Way ahead of you.

We're all familiar with KPI (Key Performance Indicator), the measurable value that demonstrates how effectively a company achieves its objectives. I couldn't find one that made intuitive sense to me, so I developed the Ultimate KPI™, a behavioral framework for tracking and encouraging constant improvement.

The Ultimate KPI is a concrete way to practice making replaceability part of your job. Remember that being replaceable doesn't mean being replaced. You're not trying to make yourself or those around you obsolete. You're not trying to put people out of a job.

In fact, irreplaceability is the enemy. Really. It renders you stuck. It means if there's no one else who can do what you do, you're a liability. If what you know only lives in your head, there's no transparency, no transfer of knowledge, and most importantly, no growth for you or the business.

Replaceability means practicing detachment, relinquishing the notion that you and you alone can "do that thing" or "solve that problem." Replaceability removes bottlenecks. It means you and your team can work on more substantive projects.

It allows growth.

The process of making yourself more replaceable involves first analyzing how you do what you do.

How do you go through various processes?

Where do you allocate your resources?

How do you spend your time?

What requires your attention but not your expertise?

We can answer those questions using The Ultimate KPI.

Think about the 20 things you do regularly: activities, tasks, projects, reconciling bank statements, leading the team, brainstorming, podcasting.

Did you know that every one of those tasks fits under one of four mindsets? You know the perspectives I talked about way back in Part IV.

Cog, Engine, Engineer, and Inventor

Quick refresher: A good way to think about the difference between Cog and Engine, then Engineer and Inventor is the difference between using your hands or your mouth. If you're engaged in Engineer and Inventor work, you're talking. You're brainstorming, you're interacting with other people. You're going back and forth. Then somebody else runs with it and makes it happen.

The Cog and Engine are literally hands-on contributions. When your hands are involved, you have to be physically situated someplace: in an office, in front of a laptop, behind a cash register.

It's important to note that the goal is not necessarily to eradicate cog activities. There are certain businesses where the cog work is the thing you do: carpentry, landscaping, bread baking, rock climbing instructor.

The business cannot operate without the Cog, because it's not just essential to the business, it is the business. So there is a place for Cog work. We just don't need to get bogged down in it.

Also, it's always going to be one task, one mindset. There is no grey area. For example, you may enjoy doing something and feel like it's clearly Inventor work, but if it *requires* you to be someplace, it's going to be the work of an Engineer. And it has to be identified as such.

Remember, each mindset contributes equally to the smooth operation of any business. But who is engaged in these activities can be the difference between a scalable business and a stalled one.

If the founder is doing Cog work, there is no leadership.

If the Engine holds on too tightly to any system or process, there is no transparency.

If the Engineer is working in the business, instead of on the business, there is no forward motion.

And if the Inventor is doing anything other than contributing a vision, the business will not grow.

How To Use the Ultimate KPI

Write down 20 tasks, activities, or projects you perform regularly.

Identify each activity as cog, engine, engineer, or inventor.

Cog: Is it manual and repetitive?

Engine: Are the tasks essential but frustrating?

Engineer: Are you working *in* the business or *on* the business?

Inventor: Does a project require your unique focus? Is there flexibility to work on it anywhere? Does it allow the freedom to explore outside the business?

Pick 16 things you will no longer do at year's end.

Use the 80/20 rule. Eighty percent must be off-boarded in order to grow.

Is the activity excessive, unneeded, unnecessary, inefficient, irrelevant?

Determine the Replacement Plan

Optimize: offload or eliminate

Automate: software system or process optimization

Outsource: delegate internally or externally

Monitor Continuous Change (Kaizen)

Monthly check-ins with yourself and your team

How many tasks are gone, reassigned, outsourced?

Set a goal, and if you don't reach it, go back and reimagine The Replacement Plan.

Printed in Great Britain
by Amazon